VANCOUVER

A History
in
Photographs

Aynsley Vogel & Dana Wyse

VANCOUVER

A History
in
Photographs

Altitude Publishing
Canadian Rockies/Vancouver

Front cover: Photographer Jack Lindsay captured this view of Vancouver in the forties from a blimp hovering over City Hall.

Back cover: This nostalgic shot captures the essence of an era when boys were made men by slicking a handful of grease through their hair. By 1958, when this photograph was taken, Vancouver was steadily becoming a major urban centre.

Page 1: In 1882, the CPR sailed 2000 Chinese men from Hong Kong to help build the railroad. They laboured for $1 a day. When the work was completed, many of them remained in Vancouver, creating the foundation for North America's second-largest Chinatown. These merchants are participating in a Chinese festival on wood-planked Dupont (now Pender) Street in 1898.

Page 2: Before the advent of the lumber industry, Vancouver was a rainforest woven with evergreens so tall and wide that, in some places, the sun never touched the earth. Here, a young settler poses in front of the first Hotel Vancouver. Built by the CPR in 1887, the hotel catered to visitors brought to the city by the new trans-continental railway. Back then, the hotel was considered too far out of town. But, as proof of the CPR's power, a new commercial district soon grew up around the Georgia and Granville location, and the young city's businesses turned their focus west.

Page 5: These boaters are enjoying a picnic at Seymour Creek in 1886. Leisure time, which was rare for the hardworking pioneers, was divided between family and prayer. When Sunday boating became popular, the Church intervened, hinting that the closer one was to land, th closer one was to God.

Canadian Cataloguing in Publication Data
Vogel, Anysley, 1967-
Vancouver: a history in photographs
ISBN 1-55153-928-4
1. Vancouver - History - Pictorial works.
2. Dana Wyse, 1965
I.Title
FC3847.37.V63 1993
971.1'33'00222
C93-091035-4
F1089.5.V22V63 1993

We acknowledge the financial support of the Government of Canada through the Book Publishing Industry Development Program (BPIDP) for our publishing activities.

Editor: Anna Payawal
Proofreader: Kim Schrader
Design: Robert MacDonald
MediaClones Inc.

Made in Western Canada
Printed and bound in Western Canada by Friesen Printers, Altona, Manitoba

Altitude Publishing Canada Ltd. gratefully acknowledges the support of the Canada/Alberta Agreement on the cultural industries.

Altitude GreenTree Program
Altitude will plant twice as many trees as were used in the manufacturing of this book.

visit Altitude's web site:
www.altitudepublishing.com

Altitude Publishing Canada Ltd.

1500 Railway Avenue, Canmore, Alberta Canada T1W 1P6

Boating Seymour Creek DEVINE Photo

Contents

In the Beginning

Along with the first prospectors and loggers to arrive on the shores of Burrard Inlet in the 1860s came the camera. An invention that predated the incorporation of Vancouver by some 20 years, it captured the remarkable rise of a remote logging town into one of the most dynamic cities on the continent. Vancouver's is a compressed and dramatic history, one that hurtled from Native longhouses to corporate towers in just one century.

The human history of the northwest Pacific coast predates both Vancouver and the camera by several thousand years. The first inhabitants in North America are thought to have been nomadic Mongolian tribes that crossed the landbridge from Asia to North America in approximately 9000 BC. Their descendants were the Coast Salish Natives who settled on the coast and along the river in the area of modern Vancouver. In this land of incredible natural riches, coastal Natives developed complex societies and advanced cultures. It is estimated that before contact with Europeans, there were more that 150,000 Natives living in what is now British Columbia. By the mid-nineteenth century, their numbers had dwindled to 60,000. Yet compared to the mere 600 non-Natives who had arrived to reinforce Great Britain's colonization of the land, the Native population was still a substantial one.

Ancestors of the Musqueam Natives were living on the banks of the Fraser River some 3000 years ago. Here, they fished for salmon, sturgeon, and eulachon. They hunted elk, deer, and seals. The surrounding forest was dense with western red cedar. Its fibrous bark and soft wood were ideal materials for weaving, carving, and building.

Squamish Natives originally wintered in villages on Howe Sound, and camped seasonally around Burrard Inlet. By the time white settlers arrived in the mid-1800s, however, some Squamish were living at Sun'ahk, on Kits Point. The nearby sandbar (today's Granville Island) had a natural spring, and a tidal fish trap. The Squamish were also living at Khwaykhway, in Stanley Park, where they celebrated the last potlatch in 1875. Across the harbour, a group called the Tsleil'waututh, ancestors of the North Shore's Burrard Natives, lived at the mouth of Indian Arm.

Opposite: The *Tartar* is stranded in shallow waters in this early 1900s scene. In 1945, a radical plan to deepen the harbour with an atomic bomb was rejected.

In the latter part of the eighteenth century, living on land they had inhabited for millennia, the Coast Salish Natives had little idea that the outside world was fast closing in on their uncharted world. But closing in it was, and from all sides. A fierce competition for the control of trading territories was taking place between Spain and Great Britain at that time. In 1775, Admiral Quadra sailed north from Mexico as far as Alaska, where he disembarked to claim the Pacific coast for Spain. In 1778, Captain Cook also sailed up the coast on the last of his charting expeditions for Britain, and was the first white person to set foot on the western shores of Canada.

It would be several years after Cook's journeys before the inland coast of modern Vancouver would be charted and explored by the Europeans. The Spanish arrived first. In 1791, Don Juan Pantoja y Arriaga became the first white explorer to enter the inland waters, and to give Georgia Strait its first European name: El Gran Canal de Neustra Señora del Rosario del Marinera (the Great Channel of Our Lady of the Rosary of the Seafarers). When he returned south to report to his superiors, it was left to second mate Don Jose Maria Narvaez to push north, past the Fraser (which he called the Floridablanca), and to anchor off Point Grey (Isla de Langara). Here, he was

Captain Vancouver records that he landed on the tip of Point Grey on June 13, 1792 at "about noon." In fact, he arrived one day earlier. He had forgotten to adjust his calendar, and did not realize his mistake until his voyage was nearly over. While exploring the area, Vancouver named Point Grey, the Strait of Georgia, Point Atkinson, English Bay, Spanish Banks, and "Burrard's Channel." Not until 1886 was his name given to the city that was founded on the shores he had charted for England.

the first to meet the Musqueam, who helped him with his charts. He was also the first European to set eyes on the future site of Vancouver.

One year later, Captain George Vancouver, a former member of Captain Cook's crew, was dispatched to the Pacific coast by King George III. He was sent to accept the surrender of the Pacific Coast from Spain at the northern outpost at Nootka Sound, and to chart the coast in hopes of discovering a Northwest Passage to China. Vancouver entered the Strait of Georgia and anchored at Point Grey (naming the land as he went). He then explored English Bay and Burrard Inlet, encountering a group of about 50 Natives, who, he recorded in his journal, "conducted themselves with the greatest decorum and civility."

A second crew of Spanish explorers, headed by Don Dionisio Alcala-Galiano and Don Cayetano Valdes, arrived at Point Grey just two days after Vancouver. When the British explorer returned from Howe Sound and Jervis Inlet, he encountered the Spanish ships. After a friendly exchange of information, he "experienced no small degree of mortification" upon realizing that the coast had been charted by the Spanish the previous year.

Point Grey's Spanish Banks were named to commemorate this unlikely meeting. And despite the work of the Spanish, Vancouver is still remembered as the first European to discover the site of the city that bears his name.

While the European sailors were busy exploring the land from the ocean, the competing fur-traders from the Hudson's Bay Company (HBC)and the upstart Northwest Company from Montreal, were desperately searching for an overland route to the Pacific. In 1793, the Northwest Company's Alexander Mackenzie was the first European to reach the west coast of Canada by land, emerging at Bella Coola. But it wasn't until the arrival of Simon Fraser at Point Grey in 1808, that an overland route for the site that would become Vancouver was finally navigated by a European explorer. Leaving Fort Fraser, he set out to follow a river he believed to be the Columbia. After a gruelling trip through treacherous canyons and torrential rapids, Fraser emerged at the Pacific Ocean. Upon determining his position, he realized in despair that he had emerged north of the actual Columbia. His situation worsened when he

was chased back upriver by an angry group of Musqueam. In disgust at "this useless river," Fraser retreated, naming it Bad River. Ultimately, the river would bear his name, and his legendary travels would stand prominently in the annals of Vancouver's history.

Once the explorers had unravelled the mysteries of Canada's western coastline, non-Native settlers would not arrive on its shores for another half-century. In 1827, the HBC trading post of Fort Langley was established several kilometres inland, near the shores of the Fraser River. In 1858, a swarm of 20,000 prospectors passed through Fort Langley to dig for gold up the Fraser. That year, British Columbia was declared a crown colony in an attempt by the British government to create law and order. In 1859, a corps of Royal Engineers was dispatched to establish New Westminster (located just southeast of Burrard Inlet, on the Fraser River) as the provincial capital. Despite the gold fever upriver, Burrard Inlet saw little more than a handful of eastbound prospectors camping out on its shores.

And so it was that Vancouver, today's metropolis of 1.5 million, "began life as New Westminster's back door."

Terminal City

The first pioneers arrived in the wilderness now known as Vancouver some 70 years after European explorers had first charted the area in the 1790s. For years the area of present-day Vancouver was a peripheral wilderness to the business of British Columbia being carried out in Victoria and New Westminster. But in the mid-1860s, a small number of permanent settlers began to trickle onto the land around Burrard Inlet, in an attempt to shape new lives in the coastal rainforest.

Brickmakers and Lumbermen

The story of the "Three Greenhorns" is among the most colourful tales of Vancouver's early history. In 1862, pioneer John Morton arrived in New Westminster with his cousin Samuel Brighouse and his friend William Hailstone. A potter from Yorkshire, Morton had apparently heard there was coal in Burrard Inlet, and was determined to start a brick-making business on its shores. That same year, the three partners purchased 223 hectares (550 acres) in the distant bush stretching between Coal Harbour and English Bay. For this land, which became known as "the brickmaker's claim," they paid $555.75. Unfortunately for the three men, bricks were not an essential item in a land boasting towering forests of the finest timber in the world. Their business failed and, for their folly, local pundits dubbed them the Three Greenhorns. Despite his entrepreneurial setback, John Morton cleared a house-site and settled down on the claim. He thus became the first settler in what would become some of the most densely populated and valuable land in the country: the West End.

Eventually, as the settlements around Burrard Inlet eclipsed New Westminster, the three investors were squeezed out by more powerful land speculators and developers. Morton searched for his fortune in California, but returned to live out his life in a West End apartment. Hailstone returned to England, convinced he had been swindled by his partners. Brighouse became a wealthy landowner and an influential citizen in New Westminster. Today, the site of Morton's original cottage is all but forgotten beneath the modern jungle of high-rises in

Opposite: John Morton was only 28 years old when he invited Samuel Brighouse and William Hailstone to purchase 223 hectares (550 acres) of timberland near Burrard Inlet in 1862. Morton, a Yorkshire potter, planned to make bricks from clay extracted from a harbour coal seam. They were branded the "Three Greenhorns" by New Westminster residents for buying such a miserable and remote tangle of wilderness. Their claim consisted of today's West End, bought at a premium price of $2.50 a hectare ($1 an acre). The brick-making scheme failed. Since locals had a backyard of free lumber, there was no demand for bricks. The West End is now one of the most densely populated areas in the continent.

Vancouver's urban core.

The next phase in Vancouver's development was forged by another entrepreneurial threesome, this time working separately and successfully. The three were Sewell Moody, Jerry Rogers, and Captain Edward Stamp, the legendary lumbermen of Burrard Inlet.

Opened in 1863, the North Shore's Pioneer Mills was the inlet's first sawmill. In 1864, after twice falling into bankruptcy, the mill was picked up by Sewell Moody. A savvy American, he was the first to capitalize on the timber riches of the Douglas fir forest that lined Burrard Inlet. With his arrival, international trade from Burrard Inlet was born, as the refurbished mill loaded the *Ellen Lewis* with lumber bound for Australia. It was a taste of things to come. Under Sew Moody's firm hand, "Moody's Mill" would hum profitably for the next 10 years.

Around the mill, the company town of Moodyville developed. It was the first settlement on Burrard Inlet. Moody's

Moodyville was one of three lumber towns to spring up along Burrard Inlet in the early 1860s. This quiet settlement, on the inlet's north shore, reflected the teetotaller sensibilities of its stern founder, Sewell Prescott Moody. For 20 years, Moodyville led Burrard Inlet in timber trade, making shingles and ship spars, and supplying masts to international navies. The wood was so pristine that architects of palaces abroad asked for beams cut from the inlet's trees.

Captain Edward Stamp, a survivor of the Crimean War, settled on the inlet in 1865. The cantankerous Stamp built the Hastings Sawmill at the foot of modern Dunlevy Avenue. Operations began in June of 1867. Within six months, he went bankrupt. Four years after arriving at the inlet, he returned to England. He is credited as the founding father of Hastings townsite, the lumber town that spread out from the mill.

stern guidance ensured that it was a temperate family town, and a role model for the rest of the area: it held the first religious service in 1865; celebrated the first wedding in 1868; opened the first school in 1870; and installed the first electric lighting north of San Francisco in 1882. When Sew Moody died in a shipwreck off the coast in 1875, he was deeply missed, and the fortunes of Moodyville began to wane.

Jeremiah Rogers arrived in Burrard Inlet from Port Alberni in 1865. Called "the greatest woodsman of them all," Rogers set up camp at Point Grey to log the monumental stand of trees that grew there. The area preserves his memory in the name of Jericho, which was originally known as Jerry's Cove. The intense physical labour of Rogers and his men produced some of the finest "Vancouver Tooth-picks" around – spars approximately 30.5 metres (100 feet) long and 61 centimetres (24 inches) square. A single tree could take two days of sawing to fell. Once felled, a tree was then hauled out of the forest along "skid roads" by

SKIDDING TEAM AND LOGGING CREW IN CAMP NEAR VANCOUVER IN THE 1880s

Opposite top: These loggers supplied raw timber to the sawmills around the harbour. In the 1880s, teams of oxen dragged enormous logs down muddy skid roads to the water's edge. Stripped poles, set roughly one metre (3.3 feet) apart, were dug into the trail, then soaked in dogfish oil to make the logs slide easier.

Opposite bottom: Natives once sailed hand-carved canoes up the Fraser River to trade at New Westminster. In 1887, Musqueam, at the mouth of the river, was the largest Native settlement. It is still occupied by the Musqueam band today.

teams of oxen. After his death in 1877, Rogers's land was logged over two more times before all the finest trees were taken. In 1884, Rogers was succeeded by Angus Fraser, who shipped flawless beams to Peking for the Imperial Palace under the request that they be 34 metres (112 feet) long and 71 centimetres (28 inches) square.

Captain Edward Stamp was a stuffy Englishman with a general disdain for the "colonials"of the inlet. For their part, locals had few nice things to say about Stamp. But while Stamp may not have made friends around his new home, he did make history. In 1865, when he founded Hastings Mill near the foot of present-day Dunlevy Avenue, he set the stage for the rise of Vancouver.

Unlike Sew Moody, Stamp had no interest in the role of benevolent dictator. Indeed his only interest was the productivity of his mill, which, within two years, became the leading lumber exporter on the inlet. Around his mill grew a rowdy, rag-tag settlement of male labourers, mostly single, who welcomed a game of cards and a drink or two.

Vancouver's begrudging founding father lasted only four years here. By 1869, Stamp's Mill was bankrupt, and Stamp had returned to England. Under new management, the mill continued for many years to be the driving force of the settlement that would grow into Vancouver.

After the obstreperous Edward Stamp sowed the seeds of the city, it was left to the garrulous inn-keeper Gassy Jack to water it.

Gastown

On a misty, fall day in 1867, a retired riverboat captain, John "Gassy Jack" Deighton, arrived on the south shore of Burrard Inlet. He intended to open a saloon, just west of the Hastings Mill property, to quench the thirst of the hardworking mill hands. His business plan consisted of a barrel of whisky and a smooth-talking manner. As one pioneer explained, "Gassy, with the craft of a Machiavelli, began to pass the loving-cup with an unstinting hand, telling that he had come to start a little business, that his means were limited and he would be glad to accept any assistance in the way of building the house. Saws and hammers fell from heaven ... In 24 hours, Deighton House flung open its doors to the public." And what a public it was! Records show that in the rough and tumble days of early Gastown, "brawlings and stabbings were frequent."

Top: Without the lumber industry, there would have been no Vancouver; without whisky, no Gastown. In 1867, riverboat pilot John "Gassy Jack" Deighton built the inlet's first saloon. A smattering of timber homes quickly followed, guarded by forest on one side and seashore on the other. Gastown was officially incorporated as Granville townsite on March 1, 1870, but locals retained the colourful name of its saloon-keeper, whose words poured as freely as the draught from his kegs. To the left, visitors relax on the verandah of Deighton's new hotel at the corner of present-day Water and Carrall streets.

Left: The Fraser residence, seen here in 1873, was one of the city's first homes. It sat in the heart of Gastown, at the corner of Cordova and Carrall. These pioneers knew true darkness. Light came from candles, oil lanterns, or from the moon. Food was prepared over a wood-burning stove, and baths were taken in steel tubs, with well water warmed by flames.

Top: Men who had had a drink too many in Granville were chained to stumps like the one on the right of this picture, and left overnight to sober up. One-armed John Clough, a drunkard himself, became the town's first jail-keeper when the local constable decided that it was more economical to hire Clough than to hold him prisoner. This is Granville in 1882.

Right: This magnificent tree loomed almost 95 metres (311 feet) above modern Granville and Georgia, where The Bay department store now stands. Before the arrival of white settlers, Natives cut trees like this with stone hammers and chisels. Pioneer Alex Fraser felled this monster using an axe and handsaw. The base measured over four metres (13 feet) in diameter. The log was cut up and sections of it were exhibited in England. James Horne stands on top of the fallen tree.

Top: In 1884, Granville was nothing more than a thin belt of ramshackle buildings cut into the edge of the forest along the shores of Burrard Inlet. Boats delivered supplies and new pioneers to these docks, and carried passengers across the water to Moodyville. On the far left is the Sunnyside Hotel, where Joe Fortes, English Bay's cherished lifeguard, first worked as a bartender.

Opposite bottom: In 1884, this pioneer family lived on Water Street, between Abbott and Carrall. This was the second laundry service operated by the Wah Chong clan, who lived in the rear of this tiny, white-washed building. Clothes were scrubbed by hand. Jennie Wah Chong was the first Asian to attend public school in the Burrard Inlet area.

Gassy ruled his rowdy gang of gambling and drinking patrons with a cajoling authority. Settler R.H. Alexander remembered that Jack "would turn out the lights and his customers at 10:30, with a reminder that they might work for him on the morrow, which they mostly did, as the bulk of their wages used to find their way into Jack's coffers."

When Edward Stamp fled back to England in 1869, Captain James Raymur took charge of Hastings Mill, and of its chaotic surroundings. His first reaction to the pioneer settlement was not entirely positive. Every bit a gentleman, Raymur could only look at the milltown in disbelief and ask, "What is the meaning of this aggregation of filth?" Over the years, the settlement around the mill evolved as a hybrid of his strict Victorian values and the lawless saloon-culture of neighbouring Gastown.

In 1870, tiny Gastown was officially incorporated as Granville townsite, although locals continued to call it by its unoffical name. It extended two blocks east from Cambie to Carrall, and two blocks north from Hastings to the waterfront. The town housed six businesses, including three saloons, two stores, and one hotel.

The next decade or so was a quiet one. Hastings Mill continued to hew large shipments of lumber out of the surrounding forest. Cargoes were sent out in all directions from the little

logging town, as ships bound for Australia, China, and Mexico dotted the inlet, awaiting loading. After work, men met at the corner of Water and Carrall streets to talk politics and swap stories under the shady tree in Maple Tree Square, behind Gassy's saloon.

While Gastown spent the 1870s "saying nothing and sawing wood," the rest of the province was embroiled in the explosive debate about the western terminus for the Canadian Pacific Railway (CPR). When BC entered Confederation in 1871, one of its main conditions was that a railway be built to connect it with the rest of the country. For the rest of the decade, the debate raged as to whether the terminus

would be in Esquimalt, or in Port Moody. Certainly, nobody considered sleepy little Gastown as a serious possibility for the terminus.

But by the early 1880s, the unassuming backwater took centre stage in the politics of Canada's railway building. Sir William Cornelius Van Horne, general manager of the CPR, dispatched a surveyor who concluded that Granville townsite would make the best port on Burrard Inlet. By 1884, Van Horne had completed negotiations with the provincial government to extend the terminus to Granville. In return, some 2430 hectares (6000 acres) of land around the town were handed over to the corporate giant. In hindsight, it seems that the CPR had already made its

St. James Anglican Church was built in 1881. Converted Natives used to pull their canoes onto the bank at Main and Alexander to attend morning sermons here. When the Great Fire overan the city in 1886, flames raced along this wooden sidewalk. Father Fiennes-Clinton rang the bell to alarm the citizens. Five minutes later, the church was ablaze, the bell molten into a sizzling lump of metal.

Top: Seated on the right, at his 1886 False Creek camp, is Lauchlan Alexander Hamilton – the first land surveyor of the CPR. He surveyed the towns of Moose Jaw, Swift Current, Calgary, and Regina before planning the roads of Vancouver. He drove the first wooden stake at the corner of present-day Hastings and Hamilton. With miraculous vision, Hamilton began the survey of the future city, marking streets and corners where there stood only trees and mudholes. He was elected alderman in the first election, and moved the resolution that eventually led to the creation of Stanley Park.

Right: In 1884, Sir William Cornelius Van Horne, general manager of the CPR, suggested that Granville be named Vancouver so that its location would be known to potential investors in England. He predicted the future importance of the city; in fact, he guaranteed it. Impressed by the deep harbour waters, Van Horne and the CPR prepared to extend the railroad past Port Moody to Granville in exchange for 2430 hectares (6000 acres) of land. The land grant handed over to the CPR consisted of all of today's Downtown core. The subsequent frenzy of land speculation catapulted Vancouver into the next decade.

decision before the talks and was merely using its leverage to exploit the little town. But at the time, no one seemed to think that this tract of land, perceived to be rather useless, was much to lose for the precious railway terminus.

Trial by Fire

Suddenly, sleepy Gastown was thrust into the world. A whirlwind of activity and development ensued. In 1885, Van Horne instructed the chief land surveyor of the CPR, Lauchlan Hamilton, to lay out the streets of the new town. Wishing to dignify it with a grander name than Gastown or Granville, Van Horne settled on the name of the man who first surveyed the area for King George III. "Hamilton," Van Horne reportedly said, "this eventually is destined to be a great city in Canada. We must see that it has a name that will designate its place on the map ...Vancouver it shall be, if I have the ultimate decision." One year later, the City of Vancouver was incorpo-

rated. It extended from Heatley Avenue west to Trafalgar Street, and from 16th Avenue north to Burrard Inlet. Four hundred and sixty-seven voters turned out in May to elect the first city council. In a flurry of development, 700 buildings sprang up in the three months between February and May, bringing the total close to 1000.

On the afternoon of June 13, 1886, the buildings disappeared even faster than they had risen. On that day, clearing fires to the west of the city were caught by a sudden wind. The flames swept toward the city, destroying everything in their wake. Father Clinton sounded the alarm, ringing the bells at St. James Church on Powell Street. Minutes later, the city exploded in fire. The church bells were reduced to a lump of molten metal. Twenty minutes later, the wind died, the fire stopped just short of Hastings Mill, and the flames sputtered out over the charred city. As the smoke cleared, the only building left standing was the Regina Hotel, at the corner of Cambie and Water streets. The weary men inside, who had survived the fire by swathing the building with wet towels and fighting off every stray spark, sat at the bar to drink "in silence and thankfulness."

From the Ashes

But not even the Great Fire could quell the spirit of this emerging boomtown. Seemingly overnight, Vancouver rose phoenix-like from its ashes. The Saturday after the fire, city council, meeting in a makeshift lean-to that

Nailed to the tree trunk at the corner of Water and Carrall streets is a sign announcing Vancouver's first election, in 1886. Here, men conspire in the shade at Maple Tree Square, discussing the two mayoral candidates, Richard Alexander, manager of the Hastings Mill, and Malcolm Maclean, a real estate dealer. Only male landowners were allowed to vote – Natives, women, and Asians were excluded. Maclean celebrated a questionable victory (many of his supporters were accused of voting twice) and was sworn in at the multipurpose customs, jail, and court building. Seats for spectators were borrowed from the prisoners. This is one of the last pictures of the city before the Great Fire roared down its streets.

On June 13, 1886, a sudden gale swept across English Bay and ignited the embers of clearing piles stacked along the north shore of False Creek. A wall of fire advanced on the city, raging into a 45 minute holocaust that consumed most of Vancouver's 1000 buildings. At least 21 people died. This photo, taken the day after the fire, shows the severity of the destruction.

served as their chambers, passed Vancouver's first building by-law. Within days, stores and hotels opened to the public. Citizens began to rebuild, determined to create a solid, organized, and handsome city in the place of the chaotic assortment of woodframe shacks and cottages that characterized the old town. The CPR benefitted from the level playing field, aggressively developing their lot sites to the west of the old city. Six months after the fire, Vancouver was back in business. The reborn commercial centre included nine saloons, 14 office blocks, 23 hotels, and 51 stores, many built in brick and stone.

Almost one year after the fire, on May 23, 1887, Vancouver's fate was sealed when the first transconti-

nental train finally steamed into the new "Terminal City." Engine No. 374 arrived to the jubilant uproar of the entire town. On May 31, the CPR-chartered S.S. *Abyssinia* set sail for Vancouver from Yokohama, filled with silk and tea. Arriving in Vancouver on June 13, the cargo was loaded onto the transcontinental train bound for Montreal, New York, and London. A record-setting 21 days after leaving Yokohama, the riches of the Orient arrived in New York. A week later, they arrived in London. For the CPR, a new era of international shipping was born. For Vancouver, a future among the world's leading ports was assured.

Around the international port and terminus, Vancouver set about creating an orderly, modern

Opposite top: Within 12 hours of the fire, rebuilding began. This time, Vancouver would be greater. Building regulations would be enforced, waterworks built. Here, the first city council meets at their temporary headquarters. Mayor Maclean is seated in the middle, surveyor Lauchlan Hamilton at the right. One of the items on the agenda that day was the purchase of a fire engine.

Opposite bottom: As Vancouver recovered from the 1886 fire, a new industry boomed – real estate. The optimistic city was expanding. Visitors remarked that it was easier to buy a plot of land than a hat. In 1887, there were 16 real estate outlets and 12 grocers. In this gag shot, a real estate agent, James Horne, sets up shop in a mammoth Georgia Street tree, partially charred from the fire.

Top: This 1887 photo of Homer and Pender streets, taken just ten months after the fire, shows Vancouver's second attempt at building a city. A giant clean-up occurred, led by the rekindled optimism of the pioneers and the prudence of insurance companies who refused to write policies until stumps had been cleared from the streets.

city. The city-building projects of the late 1880s included the clearing of streets, the laying of sewage systems, and the channelling of water from the pristine reservoirs of the North Shore lakes. Electric lighting illuminated city streets. Electric streetcars appeared, serving Downtown and the West End, and helping to develop the early suburbs of Mount Pleasant and Fairview. The tiny city revealed its aspirations to grandeur by opening the Imperial Opera House, which hosted such luminaries as Sarah Bernhardt and Mark Twain, and by establishing the 405 hectare (1000 acre) Stanley Park. By comparison, New York's Central Park measures 340 hectares (840 acres).

The old city centre was located around East Cordova and Hastings streets, and included most of the civic buildings, such as city hall and the court-

house. As the city grew, fierce competition developed between the old East Side interests (headed by local businessman and politician David Oppenheimer) and the newly emerging West Side interests (controlled by the CPR). The CPR's first shot in the war to unseat the old city centre was the 1887 construction of the first Hotel Vancouver, "way off in the woods," at Granville and Georgia. The railway used its considerable clout to draw others west, developing the exclusive West End for the city's elite and convincing businesses like the Hudson's Bay Company to set up shop across from its hotel. Over the years, the city developed between these two competing poles. The ongoing rivalry would survive until World War I, when the city centre was finally consolidated west of the original townsite.

First Train in Vancouver

Above: British Columbia joined Canada in 1871, on the condition that the province be linked by rail to the east coast. At 12:45 pm on May 23, 1887, Vancouver made history when Engine No. 374 pulled the first transcontinental CPR train into Coal Harbour, at the foot of Howe Street. Thousands came to greet the steam locomotive. The isolation of the west coast was finally over.

Opposite top: In 1835, the S.S. *Beaver* arrived from England to begin its 50 year service for the Hudson's Bay Company (HBC). The first steamship of the Pacific coast, the S.S. *Beaver* solidified the HBC's dominance of the fur trade, pushing through impossible waters to beat other traders to Native villages. It carried goods from New Westminster and the Burrard Inlet to the main trading post on Vancouver Island. In 1888, this side-wheeler was wrecked on the rocks beneath Stanley Park's Prospect Point.

Opposite bottom: In a scene resembling a Wild West movie, an 1890 Dominion Day parade moves down Cordova Street, the main retail centre at that time. In the foreground, a British Union Jack waves from a horse cart.

Top: In the harbour, high-masted ships are decorated for Dominion Day (July 1) in 1889. On the right is Granville Street in its infancy of commercial development. A rainforest covered these empty lots only a few years earlier.

Middle: This 1890 view over Granville Street's CPR Park shows the concentration of houses in the West End. At the harbour's edge ran Blueblood Alley, the West Hastings row of mansions built by wealthy CPR executives.

Bottom: In 1890, Granville Street separated the fine residential area to the west from the developing commercial region to the east. At CPR Park, left, guests from the Hotel Vancouver played tennis or lounged in the gazebo. The tiny building across the street was a liquor store. To its right, on the corner of Granville and Georgia, rests the future site of The Bay.

Top: In the beginning, Vancouver swarmed with optimistic single men and husbands who ventured ahead to find opportunities for their families. These anonymous pioneers capture the rusticity and the spontaneity of boomtown Vancouver, where men made fortunes logging or land speculating one day, then lost it all in a poker game the next. At the bedside in this 1890 bachelor's shack, photographs remind these rough hands of more civilized times back home.

Right: Deadman's Island, near the tip of Brockton Point, was a haunting sight to white settlers in the 1800s. The Salish rested their dead in carved wooden boxes high in the branches of the island's cedars. In 1888, the city erected the Pest House, a smallpox hospital lined with beds of sick prostitutes. Once the proposed site of a sawmill, an amusement park, and an industrial centre, the island now houses the HMCS Naval Reserve, built during World War II.

The Golden Years

In 1893, a chill fell over world markets. With its emergence as an international port and shipping centre, Vancouver was now vulnerable to the tensions of the global economy.

For Vancouver, the worldwide economic downturn was heightened by the disastrous local flooding of the Fraser Valley in 1894, which inundated valuable agricultural land. For almost five long years after 1893, the once irrepressible

This 1888 Cordova Street business was founded by Ontario-born Richard Winch, who sold fresh deer and grouse hunted in the nearby forest. Winch went on to make his fortune exporting canned salmon, and imported the city's first Rolls Royce in 1910.

Margaret Ormsby, "mining madness seized Vancouver, supplies of staples were rounded up, dogs broken into harness ... and stranger sights than ever before were to be seen on the skid road. Everyone from tea merchant to huckster prospered ..." It was a brief but resonant boom. By the end of 1898, the Klondike rush was over – yet Vancouver's heyday had just begun.

Land for Sale

The turn of the century heralded an age of unprecedented growth and development for the city of Vancouver. From a population of around 10,000 in 1890, its populace grew exponentially to 100,000 in 1910. The spirit of frontier boosterism had returned. Real estate speculation took on a fever pitch, and everyone joined the land lottery. The rich flipped lots as quickly as they bought them. Working men built up their stake to join the fray. Many were swept from rags to riches. A telling number is that of real estate agents, which grew from a modest 50 in 1900 to an astounding 650 a decade later.

One of the more notable figures to capitalize on the great land grab was renowned author Rudyard Kipling, who visited Vancouver in 1889. Kipling purchased a lot in the city,

optimism of the 1880s was deflated by hard realism.

Gold!

But Vancouver wasn't ready to give up its pioneer spirit just yet. In 1897, gold was discovered in the Yukon; and, once again, anything was possible. Klondike fever knocked Vancouver out of its doldrums. According to historian

Opposite top: The first Granville Street Bridge, seen in the foreground, was built in 1889 (two years before this photograph was taken). The CPR trestle bridge is in the distance. At this time, the waters of False Creek stretched east to Clark Drive. Granville Island, built from silt dredged from the creek bed, would not appear until 1916. In the left corner stands the Squamish village of Sun'ahk.

Opposite bottom: The Cambie Street Bridge, shown here in 1904, was opened in the summer of 1891. Supported by thick, wooden piles driven into the bed of False Creek, it connected the Cambie Street trail to the downtown peninsula. The tiny bridge supported wagon, pedestrian, and horse traffic, and was used by a neighbouring sawmill to move logs from shore to shore. False Creek never saw the high-masted ships the bridge builders imagined. Thus, the hand-cranked drawbridge was lifted only once a year, simply to test its mechanism. The present-day Cambie Street bridge was opened in 1985.

Top right: The discovery of Klondike gold in 1897 rescued Vancouver from a terrible depression. Thousands of gold-diggers with grimy fists full of dollars fell into the city. Rooming houses and hotels were packed with prospectors from Europe, the United States, and Eastern Canada. Local merchants hit their own paydirt by outfitting these nugget hounds with everything from mule teams to teaspoons. When the gold rush was over, many of the fortune-seekers settled in Vancouver.

Bottom right: Vancouver photographer Phillip Timms was drawn to the postcard craze of the early 1900s. He photographed anything that stood still, including this Water Street store, where one could buy anything from a mousetrap to a potato masher.

and learned the rules of the real estate game: "You order your agent to hold [your lot] until property rises, then sell out and buy more land further out of town ... I do not see how this helps the growth of the town ... but it is the essence of real estate speculation." With land titles flying back and forth, new suburbs opening, and buildings springing up, it was a heady time for Vancouver.

In the years before World War I, the real estate boom fostered a host of fine buildings that remain today as valued civic landmarks. At the close of the century, both the Christ Church Cathedral and the Cathedral of Our Lady of the Holy Rosary were erected Downtown as

Opposite top: In 1902, the Birk's Clock (originally Trorey's Clock) stood on the corner of Hastings and Granville, its first location. It was moved to Granville and Georgia in 1913, when Henry Birk took over Trorey Jewellers.

Opposite bottom: In this early 1900s Hastings Street scene, it appears as if the streetcars are on the wrong side of the tracks. In fact, Vancouver practiced the British left-hand rule until January 1, 1922, when all traffic switched to the right-hand system. By 9 am that day, the city had fallen into a state of panic, with locals fearing that the population would shrink as a result of accidents caused by disoriented drivers. Fortunately, the city adapted quickly. Streetcars doors were also moved from the left- to the right-hand side so that passengers could board from the opposite side of the street.

Top: Before bridges connected the North Shore to Vancouver, steamboats like the *Clayburn*, shown here at a CPR wharf in 1906, carried passengers back and forth across the harbour and provided a crucial link. Ferry service to North Vancouver ended in 1958.

Bottom: Horse-drawn wagons used to deliver coal door-to-door to houses in the West End. The slabs of stone on the right may have come from the rock quarry in Queen Elizabeth Park. This is the corner of Robson and Cambie in 1906.

Opposite top: Though the 1910s saw the refinement of the city, there were still large areas of forest to be cleared. This Powell Street hiring agency arranged contract work for loggers in 1911.

Opposite bottom: The boom years of the early 1900s saw improvements to the city's physical structure. These workers are building cement sidewalks on Georgia, near Seymour.

Top: Three decades after "Gassy Jack" Deighton built his first wooden saloon near this Water Street junction in 1867, sturdy stone buildings stood in a perfect row: proof of the resilience of a city that had witnessed a major fire.

Right: The clackety-clack of iron-shoed horses once announced the arrival of the latest magazines. Automobiles were rare in turn-of-the-century Vancouver, and some areas of the city still maintained water troughs for horses.

centres of worship. Soon after, financiers like the BC Permanent Loan Company and the Canadian Imperial Bank of Commerce built their classic temple banks along the new financial streets of West Hastings and Pender. The Sun Tower and the Dominion Trust Building were impressive signatures of progress, each in its turn boasting the title of tallest building in the British Empire. Just before World War I, the CPR built an elegant new Hotel Vancouver to replace the original structure. Of this second hotel, which was demolished in 1949 and replaced

Top: This group is waiting for a streetcar at the corner of Broadway and Main in 1908. In the 1900s, Mount Pleasant was home to settlers who were attracted by the employment opportunities in the factories of False Creek.

Bottom: In 1890, when the CPR created the subdivision of Fairview, a decent plot of land could be bought for under $400. Streetcar service, extended the next year, delivered new settlers. By 1900, this was the fastest growing area in Vancouver. This photograph of Fairview was taken in 1910.

Opposite top: When these Fairview frame houses were built, False Creek was advertised as having a very fair view. As sawmills and shipyards moved onto the shores, the waters became a polluted slough. So extensive was the damage that the city considered filling in the creek. It was not until the late 1970s that industrial False Creek was rescued from pollution and decay. Now, Fairview boasts office buildings and condominiums.

Opposite bottom: In 1909, James Quiney was the only resident in the Fourth and Dunbar area. He bought some property at nearby Fourth and Waterloo, shown here, in order to sell it to developers. Streetcar service played a powerful role in the development of the city, carting new builders to previously isolated areas.

by a parking lot, local writer Michael Kluckner has said "the quality of the exterior stone carving and interior finishing has not been equalled in the city since." Formidable civic buildings such as the grand Carnegie Library at Hastings and Main, and the stately courthouses at Georgia and Howe, reflected the city's growing stature.

In the heat of real estate speculation, Vancouver expanded outward. Subdivisions from Point Grey to Grandview were neatly parcelled into lots and sold. City bridges reflected this expansion. The Westminster Avenue Trestle was refurbished in 1909 to give increased access to Mount Pleasant and areas south. Also in 1909, the new and improved Granville Street Bridge, so instrumental to the success of the CPR's exclusive Shaughnessy Heights development, was opened by Earl Grey. In 1912, the four-lane, medium-level Cambie Street Bridge connected Downtown Vancouver with Fairview and Mount Pleasant. The first Georgia Viaduct stretched east from Downtown, improving access to Main Street and the East Side neighbourhood of Grandview.

The Age of Elegance

For the city's rich, the Golden Years between 1900 and 1914 were a time of palmy Edwardian elegance. In the CPR-controlled West End, the city's growing upper class fashioned a privileged world of proper British comforts and sensibilites. Fantastic mansions, surrounded by clipped hedges and holly bushes, sprang up along Davie, Denman, and Robson streets. Gabriola, the residential showpiece of sugar baron Benjamin Tingley Rogers, was one of these homes. A stately Victorian manor occupying two lots at Davie and

Opposite: When 24-year-old Benjamin T. Rogers announced his plans to build a sugar refinery in Vancouver, he received the same enthusiastic support that the pioneers had extended to the CPR. The refinery was a success. In 1900, already a very wealthy man, Rogers commissioned the glamourous Gabriola Mansion. Named after the island where some of the structure's rockwork originated, it featured 18 fireplaces and cost $25,000. The building still stands at the corner of Davie and Nicola streets, where it now houses a restaurant.

Top: By the turn of the century, Vancouver was showing signs of sophistication. West End society ladies hosted tea parties and entertained guests in ornate parlours, such as this one.

Nicola, Gabriola was designed by prominent architect Samuel Maclure, and was reported by local newspapers to have cost $25,000 – "probably twice as much as the next best residence in the city." Inside Rogers's palace was elaborate wood panelling imported from England, 18 fireplaces, opulent stained glass, and the city's first concrete basement.

According to Vancouver's *Elite Directory* of 1908, more than three quarters of the city's certifiably "elite" lived in the West End. It was a haven that allowed the upper crust to enclose themselves in an insular and genteel world against the surrounding wilderness. For women, this world revolved around "at home" days and garden parties, which were held in a different part of the neighbourhood on each day of the week. For men, life outside of business revolved around exclusive clubs, such as the Terminal City Club, the Vancouver Lawn and Tennis Club, the Vancouver Yacht Club, and, most sanctified of all, the Vancouver Club. For West End children, there were, of course, the private schools.

With the intense pace of development in the city, the West End, once considered "out of town,"

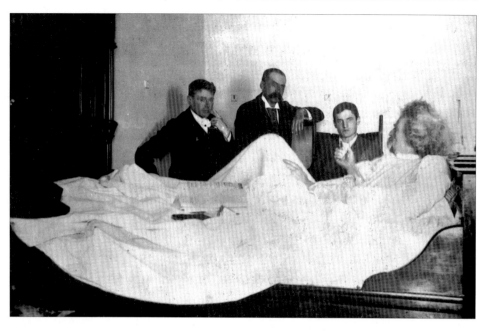

Top: In the summer of 1895, American writer Mark Twain delighted audiences at the 1200-seat Vancouver Opera House. Stricken with a terrible cold, Twain attempted to recuperate in his Hotel Vancouver suite.

Left: The CPR's original Hotel Vancouver, on the left, serviced distinguished visitors for over 25 years. In 1912, preparations began for a second Hotel Vancouver, which would replace this one.

Right: The energy with which the pioneers had built Vancouver was renewed as the city waltzed into its golden years. Vancouver had evolved into a fine metropolis where, finally, a woman could wear a dress without getting her hem dirty. These couples at a dance hall in 1909 reflect the new refinement of the city.

Opposite: Pauline Johnson, the celebrated poet and performer who was known as the "Mohawk Princess," lived in the West End in the early 1900s. She left her mark on the city by naming Stanley Park's Lost Lagoon, where she loved to canoe. In Johnson's days, the lagoon was not landlocked, and it moved with the tides of the harbour. When she went to paddle there one afternoon, the tide was out. Her favourite place was "lost."

Top: In 1904, the completion of Woodward's, a new department store, secured Hastings Street's position as an important retail centre. In one of the specialty shops near Hastings, pictured here, locals could buy a good cigar, a pair of imported leather shoes, or a child's bonnet.

Middle: Governor General Earl Grey sat in the first car to be driven over the new steel-structured Granville Street Bridge, which was opened on September 6, 1909. It was replaced in 1954 by the present-day bridge.

Bottom: The Duke of Connaught, Canada's governor general in 1912 and son of Queen Victoria, pins a medal on a proud boy scout at Hastings Park.

Top: The Industrial Building was the pride of Vancouver when the first exhibition opened at Hastings Park in 1910. Five thousand people listened as the prime minister, Sir Wilfred Laurier, christened the fairgrounds, the predecessor to the Pacific National Exhibition (PNE). Merchants sold horse medicine and demonstrated the electric water heater. The arcade featured dancing girls.

Opposite: Bathing wear has long been a controversial debate in Vancouver. These women are observing the 1890s by-law that banned swimming or bathing in public waters without a bathing suit extending from the neck to the knees. In 1914, the Vancouver Parks Board prohibited flesh-coloured bathing suits at public beaches. In the 1930s, these regulations relaxed, and men's briefs shrunk to seven centimetres (three inches) above the navel. By the late 1960s, bathing suits were not the only things that had changed: Vancouver had become internationally renowned for Wreck Beach, its nudist retreat at Point Grey.

soon fell under urban pressure. Luckily for the rich, the CPR was developing the even more rarefied Shaughnessy Heights neigbourhood on the southern rise above 16th and Granville. When the highly restricted and costly lots were offered for sale in 1910, wealthy buyers lined up around the block to purchase their share of the land touted as the most exclusive residential area west of Mount Royal and south of Nob Hill.

A Life of Leisure

The elite were not the only ones enjoying the benefits of a prospering Vancouver. In these mild, coastal climes, leisure was a commodity increasingly enjoyed by people of all walks of life. When

Vancouver kicked off its first annual summer fair at Hastings Park in 1910, 68,000 people in a city of 65,000 paid the 50 cents to enter the gates. Clearly Vancouver was ready to enjoy itself.

The focus of much of the city's year-round recreation was beautiful Stanley Park. The huge, forested promontory at the mouth of Burrard Inlet was originally set aside as a bulwark against a feared US incursion into the British colony. One of the top priorities of Vancouver's first city council was to request the use of what was then a federal military reserve as a city park. The proposal was advanced by CPR land surveyor Lauchlan Hamilton, and it is said that the CPR lobbied for the

park in order to make their West End developments more lucrative. Regardless of the motive, Stanley Park was officially dedicated by Lord Stanley in 1889 "to the use and enjoyment of people of all colours, creeds and customs for all time." And it quickly became the pride of all Vancouver.

Stanley Park was the place for summer strolls and bicycle rides. The tremendous Hollow Tree was a prime attraction, with all manner of tourists having themselves photographed inside its massive trunk. The towering grove of Douglas fir and western red cedar, known as the Seven Sisters, was also a favourite spot, giving visitors a chance to see the "giants of the forest."

Early on, a lone black bear kept by the first park ranger became the first inhabitant of the Stanley Park Zoo. Henry Avison, the park ranger's son, remebered that: "one sunny Sunday afternoon, the wife of the Methodist clergyman approached the bear ... and poked it in the ribs with the point of her umbrella. The bear took umbrage, and took a swift swipe at its molester ... and, in the twinkling of an eye, there was more than her slip showing." Shortly thereafter, a bear pit was constructed to protect the decency of park visitors. In 1912, the zoo was further expanded when a British landscape architect, T. Mawson, laid out the winding paths and gardens that exist today.

Top: The name of Stanley Park was kept a secret until its official opening by Mayor David Oppenheimer on September 27, 1888. Until then, the dense forest had been preserved as a military reserve to defend the capital of New Westminster from the rear. This arch at the entrance to the park was built from cedar trees taken from the West End.

Opposite top: Calcined white clam shells dug from a Salish midden were used to pave the original streets in Stanley Park. Parasols and hats were a must for women at the turn of the century; a suntan meant only one thing – the lady was a labourer.

Opposite bottom: These women study a sign that reads, "Bicycles and Carriages Keep Left." Automobile access was restricted in Stanley Park in the early 1900s due to "horses taking flight." Stanley Park's serenity, captured here, would have been destroyed had a proposed rifle range not been vetoed in 1889 out of concern for pedestrians.

STANLEY PARK. VANCOUVER. B.C.

Opposite: In the beginning of this century, the Sutherland Sisters, a septette of chestnut-tressed ladies, appeared in drugstore windows, brushing their waist-length hair to promote a line of hair tonics. It is speculated that the famous stand of Douglas fir and red cedar in Stanley Park was named for these popular women. Another legend claims that when the park was opened in 1888, Vancouver had only seven girls between the ages of 10 and 18; and that these evergreens guarded their favourite spot to play. Constant traffic around the trees caused their root system to compact and, in 1943, they died. In 1951, the Parks Board declared the decaying Seven Sisters a hazard and had the trees cut down. All that remains is a line of stumps. It is not known what became of the Sutherlands.

Top: The Hollow Tree in Stanley Park was one of the most photographed city landmarks in the early 1900s. Businessmen boasted their success by posing near the tree with their new steam-powered automobiles. Proud mothers flaunted the size of their families by linking hands with their daughters and circling the 18 metre (60 foot) girth of the giant red cedar.

Other recreational spots in Stanley Park included the Vancouver Rowing Club, and the Royal Vancouver Yacht Club. Both established club-houses at Coal Harbour in 1905. The clubs were social and recreational centres for the privileged classes. The Brockton Point Athletic Grounds (today's Brockton Oval) was the site of popular lacrosse matches and bicycle races. For musical entertainment, locals spread out on the grass around the bandstand, at the site of present-day Malkin Bowl.

Just outside of Stanley Park, on Georgia at Gilford, was the Horse Show Building. Constructed in 1898, and demolished in the 1960s, the Horse Show Building

was the second largest structure of its kind in North America, after New York's Madison Square Gardens. The annual equestrian shows were prime places for the West End elite to see and be seen. In 1911, the nearby Denman Arena became the first in Canada to house an artificial ice rink. The Vancouver Millionaires won the Stanley Cup there four years later.

Summers by the Sea

At the opposite end of Denman was English Bay Beach. Skirting Vancouver's most popular swimming waters, the beach was the liveliest spot to spend the long summer days. Swimmers had been drawn to its shores since the 1880s, but it was not until the turn

Top: Lumberman's Arch, erected in 1913, marks the site of *Khwaykhway*, a vanished Salish village. In 1875, 2000 people attended the last potlatch held on this beach. A smallpox epidemic forced the relocation of the Natives in 1888. In 1900, the Parks Board bought all but one of the last Native homes for $25 and, fearing contamination, burned them to the ground.

Left: The Stanley Park Zoo was born when park ranger Henry Avison chained a bear cub to a stump. In the 1900s, several Vancouverites kept pet bruins. Mother bears were often shot or trapped in nearby forests, the abandoned cubs adopted by local residents.

Top: Prospectors en route to the 1858 gold rush once pitched their tents for a month at Stanley Park's Second Beach before heading to the Fraser River. These frolickers enjoy the same beach in 1906.

Right: Barbados native Joe Fortes arrived in Vancouver in 1885, and worked as a bartender at the Sunnyside Hotel. He watched Vancouver develop from a whisky town to an international port lined with streetcars and movie houses. Fortes lived in a small cottage on the beach near the site of the present-day Sylvia Hotel. For over two decades, he served as the official lifeguard of English Bay, teaching a generation of Vancouver children how to swim. More remarkable than his kindness was the courage that shaped his life. After rescuing terrified pioneers in the Great Fire, Fortes went on to save hundreds of swimmers at English Bay.

Top: David Oppenheimer, wearing a top hat on the right, succeeded Malcolm Maclean as Vancouver's second mayor. He purchased some land that stretched between the streets of Carrall and Gore, cleared it for building, and encouraged settlers to resist the CPR's westward pull. In this 1892 scene, Oppenheimer rides the *Senator*, a steam tugboat that delivered both mail and passengers to settlements along the Burrard Inlet.

Opposite top: The spring of 1905 saw the city's first dog regulation. Apparently, bathers could no longer tolerate the habits of wet canines (shaking themselves dry) on the beach. In the background is the English Bay Bathhouse. It housed 116 changing rooms and was built in 1905 for $6000. In 1939, it was home to the city's first aquarium.

Opposite bottom: These floats – which served as a boat launch, fishing spot, and diving base – were joined to the towering English Bay Pier that stretched 92 metres (100 yards) into the ocean. Seen here in 1913, the pier was demolished in 1938. To the left of the bathhouse lies the corner of Denman and Davie streets.

of the century, when the Davie streetcar shuttled in crowds from all over the city, that English Bay came into its own. The first bathhouse – with changing rooms topped by a broad, shady verandah – was opened in 1905, then enlarged and refurbished in 1909. The bathing pier was another amenity of English Bay's heyday. Extending well into the waters of the bay, it was the spot to promenade on summer evenings. At the foot of the pier, fashionable couples romanced the night away in a glassed-in dancehall called The Prom. Back on shore, bands entertained at the Alexandra Park bandstand, while the Imperial Roller Rink catered to the pre-war roller skating craze.

Of all who thronged to English Bay, the man most devoted to the beach was honorary lifeguard Joe Fortes. Five years after arriving from Barbados in 1885, Fortes settled on the English Bay waterfront in a squatter's shack. He was a permanent fixture on the waterfront for the next 30 years, and it is said he left only to attend Sunday mass. Day and night, amid a gaggle of devoted children, he supervised the beach as its self-appointed lifeguard and swimming teacher. "And so it is," wrote prominent local writer Ethel Wilson, "that there are Judges, and Aldermen, and Cabinet Ministers, and lawyers, and doctors, and magnates, and ordinary businessmen, and grandmothers, and prosti-

Top: It was beavers, not labour unions, that troubled the lumber industry in 1867. Fresh water from Trout Lake was carried by long, wooden flumes to Hastings Sawmill to power the steam-driven machinery. The mill encountered an unexpected problem – beavers – who constantly dammed the mouth of the flume. Silly Billy Frost became Trout Lake's first resident when he was sent by the mill to regulate the animals' building activities. Here, skaters enjoy a 1905 winter at the lake.

Left: In this 1903 vista from Grouse Mountain, two climbers rest high above Burrard Inlet. Over a century earlier, Captain George Vancouver, a British explorer, passed through the inlet's first narrowing and into these silent waters. He was greeted by 50 Natives in dug-out canoes; the Natives threw white feathers on the water as a sign of friendship. Vancouver spent only one night on these shores, and would never know that this great city would one day bear his name.

Opposite: Scottish settler George MacKay was in his sixties when he and two local Natives built the first Capilano Suspension Bridge, 70 metres (230 feet) over Capilano Canyon, in 1889. Constructed from cedar planks and hemp rope, the bridge was a source of pleasurable terror to vertigo-stricken sightseers. By 1904, MacKay's bridge had disintegrated, and the first of three wire bridges (seen here in 1905) was built at the same location. The current bridge was erected in 1956.

tutes, and burglars, and
Sunday School superin-
tendents, and dry-cleaners,
and so on whom Joe Fortes
taught to swim, and they
will be the first to admit it
... He was greatly loved and
he was respected." Fortes
rescued over 100 swimmers,
and taught even more.
When his beach home was
threatened with destruction
during squatter evictions,
public outcry forced the
city to spare his cottage. It
was moved across the street
to Alexandra Park, where
he lived out his life. Shortly
after his death in 1922, a
marble drinking fountain
was installed at the park in
his memory. The bronze
plaque set into the fountain
was inscribed with the
simple phrase, "Little
Children Loved Him."

The Disenfranchised

For those residents of
Vancouver whose cultures
diverged from the domi-
nant culture, the Golden
Years revealed their darker
side. Stanley Park's dedica-
tion to those of "all colours,
creeds, and customs" was
pleasant rhetoric that
masked the inherently
racist climate of the times.
Indeed, Chinese, Japanese,
Native, and East Indian
residents were not even
allowed to vote for the city
council that created Stanley
Park. It would take more
than half a century for
them to be granted that
right.
  Race was long an
explosive labour issue in
Vancouver. The white
working class objected to
the willingness of non-
white labourers to work for

Top: These Native mothers wait for a
boat at a Vancouver wharf, in 1903.

Opposite: This solemn group poses at
Alexander Beach, near the foot of
Columbia Street, in 1898. While these
Natives had adopted the European
style of dress, they maintained old
customs. With tents pitched on the
shore of the Alexander Street
warehouse district, they set salmon
nets from their long canoes.

lower wages. And although the ruling class appreciated the cheap labour, the hiring of non-white workers often embroiled them in public relations fiascos. The mayoral candidate who lost the city's first election in 1886 was denounced for his hiring of Chinese employees. The city's first major race riot erupted in 1887, when angry white workers descended on a Chinese work camp. Afterwards, the mob was congratulated by local papers for leaving "only five Chinese in town." Two years later, when influential industrialist B.T. Rogers negotiated the opening of his sugar refinery in Vancouver, one of the city's main conditions was that he hire whites only.

Land ownership was another problem for Vancouver's minorities. When Vancouver was incorporated, Natives were not allowed to buy property, period. Many of the city's better neigbourhoods, including Point Grey, Shaughnessy Heights, and, later, the British Properties, enforced restrictions against non-white ownership. Many private landholders simply refused to sell to non-whites. It was against this backdrop that Vancouver's visible minorities lived through the Golden Years. Ghettoized, they developed their own communities within the larger city.

British Columbia was the only province in Canada whose government did not negotiate treaties with the indigenous Native population before appropriating their land. After years of broken promises regarding land settlements, in 1906 Joe Capilano, an eminent Native chief, led a delegation of fellow leaders to London. There he spoke with the "Great White Chief," King Edward VII, to air grievances about the treatment of Natives in the province. When Capilano disclosed that he and the king had discussed the return of traditional hunting grounds to the Natives, he was accused of "inciting the Indians to revolt."

The following year, the city experienced a pause in its economic advance. The brief decline sparked an intensification of racism. The Asiatic Exclusion League assigned blame for

Top: Chief Joe Capilano, fifth from the left, was a remarkable bridge between Native and European cultures. Born in Squamish in 1850, he lived his first 15 years in the forest, moving to Moodyville in 1865 to work in the mill. In 1895, he became chief of the Squamish. A clever and commanding speaker, Capilano began a crusade for Native rights that would last his entire life. In 1906, Chief Capilano led the first party of West Coast chiefs to London, where he presented his concerns to King Edward VII. Upon his return, he was accused of "inciting the Indians to revolt," when he claimed that the "Great White Chief" had promised to return traditional hunting grounds to the Natives.

Opposite bottom: In 1912, 10 street arches were built along the parade route that was to be taken by the Duke and Duchess of Connaught, who would open the new Connaught (now the Cambie Street) Bridge. The Chinese community erected this magnificent seven storey arch at Pender and Carrall to welcome the royal couple.

Right: In 1882, the CPR sailed 2000 Chinese men from Hong Kong to help build the railroad. They laboured for $1 a day. When the work was completed, many of them remained in Vancouver, creating the foundation for North America's second-largest Chinatown. These merchants are participating in a Chinese festival on wood-planked Dupont (now Pender) Street in 1898.

the downturn to Vancouver's non-white workers. On September 7, 1907, the league held a rally and march that was attended by more than 30,000 citizens. After racist denunciations were vented in speeches by prominent locals, a mob of some 15,000 set out for Chinatown, where they smashed windows, looted stores, and beat any Chinese person who crossed their path. Following this, they headed for Japantown, where they were beat into retreat by the forewarned community. It remains the worst race riot the city has ever seen. Compensation was made for damages, but anti-Asiatic protesters ultimately won immigration restrictions. A *New York Evening Post* editorial summed up the situation in an editorial entitled, "Vancouver BC – Yes, 10,000 BC."

In 1914, Vancouver's xenophobia was turned against immigrants from India. Indian citizens were British subjects and therefore could not be banned from entering Canada, a member of the British Commonwealth. To get around this, a technicality was devised to deny East Indians entry into the country unless they came by direct passage from their place of origin. To protest this, a local Sikh, Gurdit Singh, chartered the *Komogata Maru* to bring 375 Sikhs to Vancouver from India. When the ship arrived in port following a stopover in Hong Kong, the Sikhs

On September 7, 1907, racial tension exploded when the Asiatic Exclusion League, accusing the Chinese of working for less than the standard rate, led a mob of 15,000 people through Chinatown's Carrall Street. Chinese citizens were beaten, and nearly every store and home was damaged. The mob also stormed Japantown, where they were met by Japanese who defended themselves with knives and broken bottles.

Racism was widespread in turn-of-the-century Canada. To curb the number of immigrants from India, a racist immigration policy stipulated that they would be granted entry only if they arrived *directly* from their place of origin. In May 1914, 375 Sikhs sailed into Coal Harbour on the *Komogata Maru* to protest this law. As their ship had stopped in Hong Kong on their way to Canada, the Sikhs, all British subjects, were ordered to stay on board – and kept there at gunpoint. Landed Sikh immigrants rallied on shore, but cramped living quarters and diminishing food supplies forced the protestors to head home. On July 23, after six weeks of languishing in the harbour, the *Komogata Maru* returned to India.

were denied entry. Despite a legal challenge, the immigration ban was upheld in the courts. Ultimately, after languishing for more than six weeks in the waters just off Vancouver's coast, the crowded ship of hungry and tired Sikhs was forced to embark on the gruelling return journey to India.

Call to War

Just 10 days after the *Komogata Maru* sailed out of port, the city's racial troubles were overshadowed by the country's call to war. Eighty percent of Vancouverites at this time were British descendants, and patriotism ran high.

The first detachment to leave the city consisted of 75 British reservists who headed for the front two weeks after World War I was declared. A score of local battalions were not far behind.

During the war, Vancouver's population dropped by 26,000. Vancouver sent a higher proportion of soldiers to France than any other city in North America. BC contributed more volunteers per capita than any other province in the country. As one Vancouver woman recalled, "There was a lot of glamour because the boys were just going over for trips; you

know, get a trip overseas and they'd be home in no time." Of all those who left, half were wounded or killed.

At home, the war transformed the city. Life and leisure were consumed by the exigencies of war. Overnight, the Golden Years became years of sacrifice and austerity. Stanley Park was fitted with naval guns. Hastings Park and the Horse Show Building served as drill grounds for volunteers. Women raised money, knitted socks, worked for charities, and, eventually, for the factories that were scrambling to meet wartime contracts. In the process, they earned the provincial vote. Vancouver bought $700,000 worth of war bonds, and donated more than $1 million to the Red Cross.

Finally, just before midnight on November 11, 1918, the armistice was announced. Despite the hour, the jubilant city took to the streets. City archivist J.S. Matthews wrote of being woken up by the sounds of factory and steamer whistles just before 1 am at his home in Kitsilano. An hour later, he recorded: "a few firecrackers and pistol shots are ringing out, and by the distant sounds I imagine the revelry in the city must be intense."

The joy would spill over into the next decade. The 1920s would see some of Vancouver's most prosperous days.

Top: On August 4, 1914, Vancouver was pulled into World War I when Britain declared war on Germany. The feared 29th Overseas Battalion of the Canadian Expeditionary Forces became known as the "Knights of the Roller Coaster" when Hastings Park served as a training ground and soldier camp throughout the war.

Opposite top: This monstrous roller coaster was built during World War I and is still in operation. Modern-day thrill-seekers joke that it is not the dips and curls that tantalize them, but the uncertainty of the ride's mechanical soundness. In the background are homes that were built during the real estate boom that graced Renfrew following the success of the first Vancouver Exhibition.

Opposite bottom: In 1915, D.W. Griffith's epic film *Birth of a Nation* was the first full-length feature to play at the Avenue Theatre, on Main Street.

Opposite top: On Halloween, 1918, *World* publisher and eight-time Vancouver mayor, Louis D. Taylor, organized one of his infamous publicity stunts. Thousands stood on Beatty Street as Harry Gardiner, the "Human Fly," scaled 103 metres (340 feet) up the World Tower using only his bare fingers. Reportedly, six weeks later, Gardiner failed at a similar stunt in the US, and died.

Opposite bottom: On November 11, 1918, Vancouverites rejoiced at the end of World War I. A civic parade wound through the downtown streets, which were lined with 25,000 cheering people. BC lost more men in this war than any other province in Canada.

Top: Professor Hewitt and his associate proudly display their "Monster Fossils" at City Hall, around the turn of the century. The bones were thought to be the remains of a great whale.

Right: Vancouver's first Orpheum Theatre was built at Pender and Howe in 1899. Shown here in 1910, this theatre pioneered the new Orpheum, which opened on Granville Street in 1927. "Fashionable vaudeville" entertained Vancouverites in the years before radio and television.

Between the Wars

The world was a changed place after the war. The 1920s brought freedom, financial gains, and happy days. Women cut their hair, shortened their skirts, and enjoyed new independence. Men donned boater hats, and pants with wide cuffs. Although Vancouver was not New York or Chicago, and was distant from the real roar of the times, its echoes did reverberate throughout the city.

A new age of expansion and progress dawned on Vancouver's streets. International stock market speculation seemed to yield endless profits, helping the rich get richer. The newly opened Panama Canal, and a dramatic rise in wheat exports, boosted shipping activities in Vancouver's port. Total exports for the city quadrupled in the years between 1921 and 1929. Vancouver also became slightly

Hastings Mill, shown here in 1919, was Vancouver's main employer until the arrival of the CPR in 1887. Built in 1865 by Captain Edward Stamp, the mill was one of the few structures to survive the Great Fire of 1886. It featured a schoolhouse and a store. In 1930, the Hastings Mill Store, Vancouver's oldest building, was floated to the foot of Alma Street. It now operates as a museum.

more industrialized, as hundreds of small factories sprang up and helped to absorb the glut of post-war unemployed. The city limits grew to subsume the suburbs of South Vancouver and Point Grey. The population rose to nearly 250,000 by the end of the decade.

Seventy percent of the nation's homes had electricity by the end of the 1920s. When technological advances like electric irons and vacuum cleaners created more free time, the radio stepped in to fill it. The greater world arrived in thousands of living rooms across the city as families tuned in to American radio shows. But the biggest freedom of all came with the automobile. Vancouver had 650 cars in 1920; within ten years, that number had ballooned to 36,500. Auto camps and the city's first drive-in restaurant, The White Spot, catered to the car craze. In 1928, the first traffic light was installed downtown.

This was the time to go out on the town and dance the Charleston. The Pantages Theatre on Hastings brought Duke

Ellington and vaudeville acts to Vancouver. But "talkies" were the coming rage. The first talking picture, *Mother Knows Best,* was screened at the Capitol on Granville in 1928. The Capitol was just one of the venues along what would become Vancouver's Theatre Row. In 1927, the luxurious Orpheum Theatre opened down the street, bringing stars like Bill "Bojangles" Robinson to town. Fashionable couples also dined on Granville, at the Chanticleer Cafe, or at Love's Grill.

While his uncle's theatre was entertaining the star gazers, local restaurant owner Peter Pantages was organizing the Polar Bears. Pantages himself never went a day without a morning dip in the frigid waters of English Bay. In 1920, he founded the Polar Bear Swim Club, which organized an annual winter swim for those who felt that once a year was enough. After the swim, Pantages and his friends would regroup for festivities at his Peter Pan Cafe, on Granville.

Another high point in the world of amateur sports came in 1928, when native son Percy Williams took the world of track and field by storm. Percy became a national hero when he captured the gold in both the 100 and 200 metre sprints at the Amsterdam Olympics.

In 1921, in his last year as governor general of Canada, the Duke of Devonshire visited Vancouver. The following year, Lord Byng took up the post as the King's representative in Canada.

Top and middle: These two views of the Downtown core demonstrate the explosive growth that shaped the city. In 1891, the population totalled 13,000. By 1923, it had passed 100,000, and the city displayed several impressive buildings.

Right: In the giddy and happy-go-lucky twenties, no fashionable man met a Vancouver spring without a good straw boater. This is a display for Robinson's Clothing Shop, in 1926.

Opposite top: On the steps is Teddy Lyons, the famous, quick-witted conductor of this BC Electric observation car. Such cars toured sightseers around the luxurious Shaughnessy mansions and around Stanley Park from 1909 to 1950.

Opposite bottom: When the *Province* newspaper moved to Vancouver from Victoria in 1898, islanders grumbled about the growing importance of the mainland community. Here, the Province Building is decorated for a 1927 Dominion Day celebration.

Top: As a growing metropolis, Vancouver could no longer survive solely on its primary resources of fish and lumber. Secondary industries, like this broom factory in 1927, operated in East End warehouses.

Right: Vancouver remembered its first fire. In 1912, a report listed Vancouver's fire department among the best in the world, matched only by Leipzig's and London's. It was the first department in Canada to be completely motorized. In 1930, Fire Hall No. 2 stood on Seymour, near Robson. It was torn down in 1957.

Opposite top: Kitsilano Beach used to be called Greer's Beach, after squatter Sam Greer. Greer's shack once stood on the site of the beach house, shown here in 1931. In 1884, the CPR claimed that they owned Greer's land. The squatter argued that he had bought the beach from two men named "Charlie and Joe," and refused to move. When Greer shot the sheriff who had been sent to evict him, he was sent to jail; the CPR eventually got their land. A saltwater pool was opened at Kits Beach in the summer of 1931, and was then largest pool of its kind in North America.

Opposite bottom: In 1791 Spanish explorer Jose Maria Narvaez became the first European to spy the future site of Vancouver when he anchored the *Santa Saturnina* in the waters here. When the Squamish Natives saw the high-masted schooner they thought that a tree-lined island had broken off from the mainland. And when they saw the pale faces, they gasped that their ancestors had returned. On Christmas Eve 1929, the government leased Spanish Banks to the city for a public beach.

Top: The Squamish fishing village of Sun'ahk was located at the south end of the Burrard Street Bridge, on land designated as part of the Kitsilano Reserve. In 1901, the provincial government supported the public opinion that the land was too valuable to be left undeveloped. The Natives were asked to move. The Squamish had no choice but to exhume their dead and abandon their ancestral site. In 1913, the BC government paid $300,000 for the 32 hectare (80 acre) strip of land. In the distance are the 1927 beachfront homes of the West End.

Bottom: Wales native David Spencer began his retail career in Victoria, selling Valentine's Day cards in the 1860s greeting card craze. In 1906, he came to Vancouver and opened a chain of department stores which would be bought by Eaton's in 1948. Here, Spencer poses with the "Bathing Girls" to promote a 1927 Kiwanis Club play.

DAVE SPENCER AND BATHING GIRLS
IN THE ATTACHED ATTACHE.
BY KIWANIS CLUB. VANCOUVER THEATRE.
NOV. 23·24·25·26. 1927.

Opposite: In 1928, the city sent young Percy Williams to the Summer Olympics in Amsterdam. On August 1, Williams captured Vancouver's first and second gold medal when he won both the 100 and 200 metre sprints. The fastest man in the world returned a hero, greeted by thousands in a parade that stretched 2.4 kilometres (1.5 miles) to Stanley Park.

Top: The newspaper astrologer, Omar, visited the city in 1932.

Right: In 1929, magician Harry Houdini stunned a crowd when he dangled from Vancouver's Sun Tower by his heels, then escaped from a straitjacket.

Top: The CPR developed the prestigious Shaughnessy Heights in 1909 and quickly attracted the well-to-do from the West End. Shaughnessy was then, as it is now, an impressive subdivision. The morning after a lavish party in 1925, Janet Smith, a Scottish nanny, was found murdered in the home of her Shaughnessy employer. She had been shot in the head and thrown down a set of stairs. In an amazing cover-up, the coroner ruled the death accidental. Although the middle-class East End blasted the police's soft handling of the rich and the extravagant lifestyles of the upper-class fell under close scrutiny, the case remained closed and the murderer unknown.

Opposite bottom: Automobiles were still rare when local photographer Leonard Frank snapped this 1919 photograph of a log bridge over North Vancouver's Seymour Creek.

Wine and Roses

In the 1920s, Shaughnessy Heights saw its most glamourous days as the well-to-do celebrated their riches. Influential old families, like the McRaes, held lavish masquerade parties in the ballrooms of their opulent mansions. The end of three years of Prohibition in 1920 was toasted in style with imported wines and spirits. A.D. McRae's wine cellar alone was said to house some 2000 bottles. Meanwhile, the younger set raced around town in their automobiles, and played tennis, bridge, and golf. They were rumoured to frolic through the night, toasting midnight skinny dips with French champagne.

In 1924, the debauchery of the rich shocked the city when Shaughnessy nanny Janet Smith was found dead in her employers' home. Her body was discovered after the couple for whom she worked had hosted an all night party. Violence, drug abuse, corruption, and police collusion were all uncovered during the extended murder investigation; but no murderer was ever convicted.

Opposite top: In the 1920s, the public began to question the importance of the Vancouver Exhibition. The land at Hastings Park was simply too valuable to be reserved for a fair. In 1923, the city demanded that the exhibition expand its operations to provide a variety of recreational activities, including a campground. Here, tourists enjoy the novelty of the Hastings Park Auto Camp, located at the foot of Windermere Street in 1924.

Opposite bottom: The 1929 stock market crash overwhelmed the city. This "hobo jungle," located at the city dump on Prior and Heatley streets in 1931, was one of four cardboard towns built by destitute men. Here, "jungleers" receive church handouts.

Top: These Depression-era men wear tags that read "United For Democracy." In the 1930s, Communist leaders gained strong support from discouraged, disillusioned, and unemployed workers.

End of the Line

Five years later, the happy days turned hungry with the stock market crash of 1929. Suddenly, the wealth of the speculators was just so much paper. And just as the Roaring Twenties sent its echoes across Vancouver, the Great Crash sent shock waves.

Vancouver barely realized what had happened, and quickly prepared for the promised recovery. Major public works projects, including the Burrard Street Bridge and the Sea Island Airport, were enthusiastically undertaken by the city. Construction by private developers continued on the masterful, art deco Marine Building; on the Royal Bank Building, the city's first bank tower; and

on the new Hotel Vancouver. In truth, however, these city landmarks were not symbols of recovery but testaments to an earlier age of prosperity. The Marine Building developers went bankrupt just after completion, selling out to the Guinness family for less than half the cost of construction. The Royal Bank Building was never actually finished according to its design, and stands today at half its intended height. Emblematic of the 1930s was the unfinished shell of the Vancouver Hotel, which dominated the skyline for more than 10 years before it was rushed to completion in 1939. The Second Narrows Bridge, knocked out of commission in a 1930 shipping accident, rusted

Top: During the Depression, Vancouver was billed the "mecca of the unemployed." Solemn men rode the trains from the prairies searching for work and shelter in the warmer climate of the West. Relief camps, paying 20 cents a day, provided a temporary solution to the crisis, but the despair would not subside for years. Mass rallies – like this one held at Powell Street's Oppenheimer Park in 1938 – saw Communist leaders attack a government that many felt had abandoned them.

Left: Bloody Sunday brought the despondency of Vancouver's unemployed to national attention. On June 20, 1938, the RCMP used tear gas and batons to expel over 100 sit-down strikers who had occupied the art gallery for a month in a demand for government relief. Led by a militant member of the Communist Party, Steven Brodie, the men would not surrender. For more than an hour they rioted on Hastings Street, smashing storefronts, and duelling with the police.

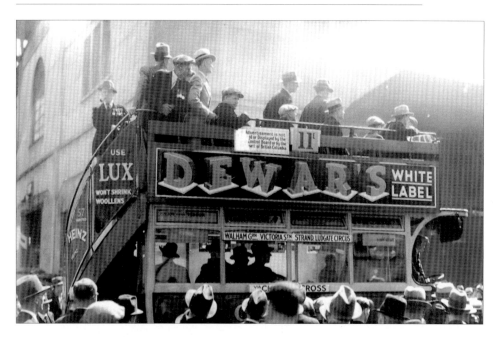

Above: 1936 was a stern time for the city. The Depression had pushed Vancouver into the depths of bankruptcy and public morale was low. Mayor McGeer attempted to fight the city's blues by organizing an extravagant celebration to mark Vancouver's first 50 years. Here, men watch from a London double-decker bus as the Golden Jubilee Parade passes.

idly for five years while awaiting repairs. Municipalites like Burnaby and North Vancouver fell into receivership.

The numbers of the unemployed and the destitute grew steadily. In the absence of a social net, the jobless held mass demonstrations in Cambie and Oppenheimer parks to draw attention to their plight. At night, men congregated in shanty towns or "hobo jungles" under the Georgia Viaduct and on the shores of False Creek. The Depression was seen as the failure of capitalism, and support for left-wing parties strength-ened, turning Vancouver into one of the most politically radical cities on the continent. In the depths of the Great

Depression, between 1932 and 1933, 15 percent of the city's population (a total of some 40,000 people) received relief payments. As the lean years wore on, Vancouver earned the dubious title of "Hobo Capital" of Canada. Its mild climate and low cost of living made it a mecca for the country's homeless and out of work.

Work and Wages

By 1935, there were some 200 work camps employing men across BC for 20 cents a day. Unrest continued to grow palpably. In the spring of 1935, 4000 men went on strike and marched on the city, demanding "work and wages." At the subsequent rally in Victory Square, Mayor McGeer arrived to read the Riot Act

Opposite top: The advent of the automobile beset Vancouver with a new problem – traffic jams. The city's existing bridge system was inadequate. In 1931, in the midst of economic despair, the Burrard Street Bridge project was lauded by the unemployed. Named after Captain Vancouver's naval friend, Sir Harry Burrard, the bridge opened on July 1, 1932.

Opposite bottom: By 1934, the West End was in the grip of a major transformation. Apartment buildings replaced frame homes, and CPR-built mansions were converted into rooming houses. These Robson Street homes once stood near the heart of modern Vancouver's shopping district.

Top: This is Commercial Drive in 1935. The character of this street was established after World War II, when many Italian immigrants settled in the East End. They established businesses and cafes, creating the "Little Italy" atmosphere for which Commercial Drive is popular today.

to the protesters. The Mounted Police then dispersed the crowds with clubs. McGeer was not amused, viewing the strike as a "prelude to a revolution to bring about a Soviet government in Canada." Three years later, the despair of the unemployed again erupted with the closure of work camps in the spring. After more than a hundred people were arrested for panhandling on city streets, a revolt occurred. The strikers occupied the art gallery and the post office, awaiting support from Ottawa. There was no response at all from the government. Again police moved in, this time dispersing the men with tear gas as well as with clubs. After this second wave of violence, public support swung in favour of the unemployed.

In the final years of the 1930s, the worst economic crisis was over for the beleaguered city. Work returned with the renewed development. In 1940, the long-awaited Unemployment Insurance Act was passed. When King George VI and Queen Elizabeth visited the city at the close of the decade, it was ready to receive them with a new, modernistic city hall, the elegant Lions Gate Bridge, and the third and largest incarnation of the Hotel Vancouver – completed just in time for their arrival.

But the biggest stimulus to the economy, another war in Europe, was just around the corner.

Top: In 1931, Vancouver welcomed Canada's first visit by Asian royalty, when Prajadhipok, the king of Siam, arrived on the *Empress of Japan*. The CPR's elegant trans-Pacific passenger service began in 1887 with the arrival of the *Abyssinia*, which brought exotic tea and silk from Yokohama. Since then, countless vessels have delivered visitors to this important international port.

Left: There are many different legends about the history of Siwash Rock. According to one legend, the rock was once a man, too clever for his own good, cast to stone by Native gods. Another version says that Native gods turned an honourable chief, who defied them for the sake of his newborn child, into the rock as a symbol of perfect fatherhood. Here, the Vancouver Natural History Society of 1932 poses in front of the rock.

Top: Coal Harbour from Stanley Park, 1935. An elegant cruiseship rests at the foot of the CPR docks where, half a century later, the five-sailed roof of the Vancouver Trade and Convention Centre would be built.

Right: The beautiful Marine Building was one of only a handful of skyscrapers in 1931 in Vancouver. Since the 1930s, city planning has centered on preserving the view of the mountains. Many building projects have been rejected so that Vancouverites could enjoy their city's unique position, wedged between mountain and sea.

Opposite: In 1918, an earthquake stopped the clock on the impressive Vancouver Block office tower, built in 1910. In 1935, Granville Street, where the Vancouver Block still stands, was already a major Downtown thoroughfare.

Top: Vancouver's Golden Jubilee celebration in 1936 saw its downtown streets decked with lights and banners. To the right is the second incarnation of the Hotel Vancouver, which opened in 1916.

Bottom: The Marine Building, built in 1929, was long Vancouver's tallest building. A symbol of jazz-era prosperity, it has been called an art deco masterpiece.

Another War

When World War II was first declared, Vancouver hardly seemed like a city at war. The conflict overseas brought a welcome economic boost to the ravaged city. Suddenly, after years of unemployment, there were more jobs than there were workers. New residents poured in from the BC Interior and the prairies. Women were welcomed into the ranks of traditionally male occupations, working at shipyards and munitions plants. Vancouver became a centre of shipbuilding in response to staggering ship orders. In the two years from 1940 to 1942, the number of shipyard employees in North Vancouver alone rose from 800 to 12,000. In total, Vancouver employed some 20,000 workers in its shipyards. The Boeing Aircraft plant on Sea Island employed 5000 workers.

Immediately after the Japanese attack on Pearl Harbour in 1941, Canada's Pacific coast city developed a siege mentality. Wartime measures were suddenly enforced – 10,000 volunteers descended on the Air Raid Protection organization; a blackout was initiated; the military took over Stanley Park; and hysteria erupted over the presence of Vancouver's Japanese community. Overnight, Japanese-Canadians, who had shown no signs of military subversion, were declared enemy aliens. The entire Japanese population was rounded up, temporarily housed in the Hastings Park Exhibition

Top: In 1937, the affluent Guinness family spent $6 million to build the Lions Gate Bridge, creating access to their new British Properties development in West Vancouver. The bridge remained a toll bridge until the government purchased it in 1963. The pair of lions at the southern end of the bridge were sculpted by Charles Marega.

Opposite top: The opening of the third Hotel Vancouver coincided with the 1939 visit of King George VI and Queen Elizabeth. Three months later, Britain and France would declare war on Germany.

Opposite bottom: The 1939 royal visit momentarily overshadowed Vancouver's economic problems. These clever entrepreneurs are selling seats to royal-watchers for a dollar each.

Opposite top: The dial telephone was not established in Vancouver until 1939. The 1940 exhibition at Hastings Park featured a demonstration of the strange, new device.

Opposite bottom: During wartime, the Vancouver Exhibition maintained operations. Two years later, the PNE would become a holding ground for 8000 displaced Japanese-Canadians.

Top: When the wealthy abandoned the West End for more exclusive locales, like Shaughnessy Heights and the British Properties, the working-class moved in. However, a high-rise apartment boom, which began in the late 1950s and continued through the 1970s, encouraged the return of the rich (who swept up suites with harbour views). Today, the West End holds the highest density of apartment-dwellers in Canada.

Bottom: Shanghai Alley, shown here in 1944, is secreted between the CPR tracks and Sam Kee's 2 metre (6 foot) wide Pender Street building. This tiny street serves as a reminder of a hostile battle between clashing cultures. It was here, in 1887, that Chinatown citizens erected a barricade to keep white race-rioters at bay.

grounds, and then shipped off to prison camps away from the coast. Japanese stock, property, and businesses, including more than 10,000 fishing boats, were seized and liquidated. Local historian Bruce Macdonald notes that the much larger Japanese population at Pearl Harbour was left intact without any treasonous repercussions. It was left to Canada, with unquestionably racist overtones, to punish those of Japanese descent for distant hostilities.

The city eventually relaxed its blackout, perhaps realizing that it was, after all, an unlikely target. Vancouver's citizens returned to the more mundane preoccupations of working hard for the boys overseas, coping with a housing shortage, and making due with rations. Leg makeup appeared in stores in the absence of nylons. Cuffs on men's pants were outlawed in an effort to conserve fabric. Meatless Wednesdays were declared, and kitchen gardens became a patriotic endeavour. Throughout all this, the internment of the Japanese continued.

News of the war's end arrived in the afternoon of August 14, 1945. At the Boeing plant, "some laughed, some were reflectively sober. Many walked uncertainly out of the open doors of Plant 3 to gaze in the direction of the siren which shattered the sunlit afternoon." V-J Day brought the weary city to the streets to celebrate the imminent return of its men from Europe once again.

Return they did, to loving families and scarce housing. But despite cramped quarters, the post-war baby boom marked the start of an era of peace-time prosperity and growth. Wartime exigencies came to an end. Women lined up for the first shipment of nylons in years. Children lobbied for an end to the candy taxes brought by the war. Canada's visible minorities were finally granted the rights of full citizens, including the vote. Japanese-Canadians were freed to rejoin their families and return to the coast. In 1988, they were compensated an average of 10 cents for every dollar taken by the government during the war.

Opposite: When Japan attacked Pearl Harbour on December 7, 1941, Vancouver declared its own war on Japanese-Canadians. Hastings Park became an impounding centre, where "enemy aliens" were ordered to surrender their cars, radios, and cameras. As the Japanese were relocated to remote work camps in the BC Interior, the Custodian of Enemy Property auctioned off their boats and businesses at deflated prices. In 1988, the government issued a formal apology to Japanese-Canadians.

Top: In 1941, Vancouver witnessed its first war-time blackout. Windows were covered with tar paper, and automobile headlights were taped to reveal only a sliver of light. Fear of a Japanese air assault gripped the city. This policeman is enforcing the dusk to dawn curfew imposed on Japantown.

Right: On August 14, 1945, headlines screamed the good news: Japan had surrendered; World War II was finally over. As a shipping centre, Vancouver's economy had actually benefited from the war overseas. With the gains made at wartime, the city embarked on a period of urban development, whose momentum lasted well into the fifties.

Lotus Land

After the long years of scrimping through the economic hardship of the thirties and the wartime uncertainty of the forties, Vancouver was more than ready to enjoy the fruits of progress brought by the fifties. The city witnessed the appearance of the first new high-rises since the late twenties. The Burrard Building was the first modern skyscraper in the city, followed one year later by the 1957

Photographer Jack Lindsay captured this view of Vancouver in the forties from a blimp hovering over City Hall. The 1912 Connaught Bridge, in the centre, was replaced by the wider Cambie Street Bridge for Expo 86, which in turn would replace some of the False Creek lumberyards seen here. Flanking the Downtown core are two of Vancouver's grandest buildings: the Hotel Vancouver, to the left, beside the Lions Gate Bridge; and the Marine Building, to the right. Above the city rest the snow-capped, twin peaks of The Lions, known to early Native inhabitants as The Sisters.

limits, while the suburbs absorbed a staggering 87 percent, doubling in size by the end of the decade. Along with the rest of North America, Vancouver's couples settled into suburban houses, continued the post-war baby boom, and drove to newly created malls (pioneered in Canada by West Vancouver's 1950 Park Royal) to shop. Televisions became the cornerstones of the new "family rooms," or "rec rooms," bringing popular American culture directly into homes across the city. Ironically, Vancouverites even watched the coronation of their new monarch, Queen Elizabeth II, on Bellingham's KVOS – the Canadian Broadcasting Corporation would not air locally until 1953.

With progress came a renewed focus on the cultural life of the city, and an array of new public projects. These included the Maritime Museum, the Vancouver Public Aquarium, the main branch of the Vancouver Public Library, and the Queen Elizabeth Theatre. In 1954, the city prepared to host the world at the British Empire Games, constructing an Olympic-size pool and the 30,000-seat Empire Stadium. The highlight of the competition was the dramatic "Miracle Mile," in which

BC Hydro Building at Nelson and Burrard. With the passage of high-density zoning laws for the West End that same year, both buildings would soon be joined by a wall of towers at their backs.

The city's population again grew with the times. Thirteen percent of Greater Vancouver's new residents settled within the city

Left: These brassieres symbolized the end of war-time restraint. In the 1940s, Vancouver sacrificed. Tea, coffee, sugar, meat, and gasoline were all rationed. Even men's clothes suffered restrictions – in order to save fabric, no pleats or cuffs were allowed. When department stores stocked nylons again in 1946, thousands of bare-legged women lined up.

Opposite top: This False Creek railyard, photographed in 1953, was part of the original 1884 land grant given to the CPR to entice its tracks westward. In 1986, when Vancouver celebrated its centennial, these tracks were lifted to build Expo 86, a first-class world exposition attended by millions.

Opposite bottom: In 1954, Vancouver hosted the British Empire Games in the new Empire Stadium at Hastings Park. There, spectators witnessed the Miracle Mile, when British sprinter Roger Bannister slipped past Australian John Landy to cross the finish line in 3:58:8 minutes. Landy burst through less than a second later. It was the first time that two men had run a four minute mile in the same race.

Britain's Roger Bannister inched past Australia's John Landy to win the race. Both men clocked in at under four minutes, setting a new world record: never before had two runners completed a mile in less than four minutes, in the same race. The event was the cover story of the premier issue of *Sports Illustrated*. The games, broadcast by CBUT, the CBC's new local station, was the first international sporting event ever broadcast across North America. It brought the city its first taste of international exposure.

1954 offered another reason for locals to celebrate. That year, Vancouver licensed its first cocktail bar. It was located on the top floor of the Sylvia Hotel. Two years later, rock and roll came to town with the 1956 performance of Bill Haley and the Comets at the Kerrisdale Arena. The show was panned by the *Vancouver Sun* as the "ultimate in musical depravity." But the fans paid no attention to the concerns of their stuffy

elders. It was the beginning of the powerful youth culture that would mark the sixties and seventies.

Against the happy productivity and consumerism of the 1950s, the Cold War played a background role. The shadow of the atomic bomb had been cast by World War II. The threat of war with the evil Soviet Union was the fodder of propagandists. Employees were screened for Communist sympathies, private citizens built their own bomb shelters, and air-raid sirens were tested. In 1953, in reaction to this rise of conservatism, students at the University of British Columbia publicly denounced McCarthyism as a "witch hunt" and Senator McCarthy himself as a

"facist," urging that he be barred from Canada.

The years of progress came with some growing pains. At the close of the fifties, Vancouver was faced with the big city problems of traffic congestion and urban decay for the first time in its history. In the following years, the city would define itself in the ways it struggled with these challenges.

The Modern Era

1960s Vancouver was a city on the cusp between past and future. Over the next 25 years, Vancouver would move beyond its role as a provincial outpost and toward its modern character as a global metropolis. It would also move away from a complete economic dependence on primary

Top: Started by the Pantages family in 1928, the Polar Bear Swim has become a chilly annual tradition in Vancouver. At precisely noon every January 1, hundreds of brave Vancouverites plunge into the frigid waters of English Bay to start the new year with a splash. This winter swim took place in 1957.

Opposite: The revitalization of Granville Island did not begin until 1978. In its decades of use as an industrial centre, the island had become dilapidated and charred from oily fires. In 1956, a seedy shantytown still existed along the waterfront, inhabited by outcasts of the Depression, who settled in these floating shacks. Living conditions were atrocious. After a typhoid scare, the city finally cast the squatters out.

Opposite top: On July 17, 1958, the Second Narrows Bridge collapsed while under construction, killing 19 men. It was the city's worst catastrophe since the Great Fire of 1886. The bridge would not be completed for another two years.

Opposite bottom: The new eight-lane Granville Street Bridge opened in 1954, replacing the swing-span bridge built in 1909. During the 1940s, Vancouverites constantly pressured city council to solve traffic jams caused by the old bridge, which was lifted whenever ships had to pass into False Creek. The new bridge stands high enough to allow boats free passage.

Top: This nostalgic shot captures the essence of an era when boys were made men by slicking a handful of grease through their hair. Vancouver had changed dramatically since its incorporation in 1886, when the ratio of men to women was two to one. By 1958, when this photograph was taken, the ratio was even. And Vancouver was steadily becoming a major urban centre.

resource extraction and shipping, forming a post-industrial economy as a service centre for western Canada.

Throughout the sixties, the city forged ahead with almost uncontrolled growth, acquiring 220 high-rises and 17,000 residential suites. Downtown, office space doubled. The West End was transformed from a collection of rooming houses and small apartment buildings to a dense urban community, housing thousands of single office workers in 30-storey towers. But Vancouver was also a city that still supported three sawmills at the edge of its Downtown core. And in the shadow of Downtown, False Creek's log-choked waters housed

the city's dismal industrial island with its host of dilapidated warehouses.

Young at Heart

While economic forces were embracing progress, Vancouver's young were hypnotized by rock music and the counterculture. Elvis Presley and The Beatles played to the disgust of reviewers and the screams of fans. As the decade wore on, the unsuspecting city came to be known as the "Hippie Capital of Canada." When some 7500 "multicoloured dropouts and draft dodgers selling hash pipes and love beads" descended on Kitsilano, Mayor Tom Campbell was unimpressed. He threatened to "shave the hippies," and

Top: Chinatown's spectacular neon displays attract many nighttime visitors. Vancouver's first neon sign was lit in 1925. Some say that Vancouver had the most linear feet of neon in the world during the 1950s. The Ho Ho Chop Suey, aglow here in 1961, is a local dining and neon institution.

Middle: The third and present-day Hotel Vancouver graces this shot of Downtown Vancouver, taken from Stanley Park in 1961. The BC Hydro Building, lit up in the right background, features a set of rooftop air chimes which play the first four notes of "O Canada" at exactly noon each day.

Bottom: Marilyn Monroe visited the city in 1961. Two years before, another Hollywood legend, Errol Flynn, died here. Since then, film and TV celebrities have kept local star-watchers happy. Billed as "Hollywood North," Vancouver has begun its own expansive film industry.

Top: These UBC engineering students are staging an anti-Communist demonstration in 1965. Although Vancouver was soon to be known as the "Hippie Capital of Canada," some of its local youth were considerably more conservative.

Middle: When the Squamish surrendered the Kitsilano Native Reserve in the early 1900s, developers fought unsuccessfully to control the land. It remained unoccupied until World War II, when the Royal Canadian Air Force built a storage depot at Kitsilano Point. In 1966, the future of Vanier Park was sealed when construction of the H.R. MacMillan Planetarium and the Vancouver Museum began.

Bottom: This 1968 panorama of the Downtown skyline was taken from Spanish Banks, across to English Bay. Vancouver, once a shacktown perched against the seashore, had now been transformed into a city of gleaming skyscrapers.

Top: When Pier B-C was built in 1927, it was a symbol of the CPR's stronghold on Vancouver's harbour. It was here that passengers embarked on the decks of the majestic *Empress* oceanliners. In 1970, when this photograph was taken, the glory of Pier B-C had long past – airplanes had replaced oceanliners as the mode of travel. Today, this is the site of the Canada Place complex.

Left: The Westcoast Energy Building on West Georgia Street reflected a growing concern of this metropolis: earthquakes. Built in 1969 (borrowing principles used to design suspension bridges), this quake-resistant structure was constructed from top to bottom. An identical building was built in Hong Kong by the same architects.

Vancouver's activists took on the world in the 1970s when a local organization, Greenpeace, agitated for peace and the preservation of the environment.

issued stern warnings that Canada's youth were not welcome in Vancouver.

Far from solving the problem, Campbell's opposition merely fanned the flames of rebellion. In 1967, Stanley Park was the site of the country's first be-in. Also that year, local peace and environment activists founded the Don't Make A Wave Committee. Soon to be renamed Greenpeace, it would grow to be the world's largest environmental organization, with more than 5 million members. An underground weekly, *The Georgia Straight* was the voice of the counterculture.

Urban Renewal

In the mid-1960s, Vancouver's city council feared the arrival of the urban stagnation being suffered by other major cities of North America. Consultants were brought in from the United States. Their recommendations included the revitalization of the urban core through the development of a modern Downtown shopping and hotel complex, as well as the construction of an urban freeway. This slated "urban renewal" would destroy the historic neighbourhoods of Strathcona, Chinatown, and Gastown.

The "Great Freeway Debate" of 1967 polarized

the citizens of Vancouver in an argument that continues in varying forms today. Pro-development supporters saw Vancouver as a burgeoning global city that had to grow and change, in order to compete fiercely in the international community. Conservationists saw the city as a relatively small-scale community whose greatest asset was its high quality of life. At the close of the sixties, the developers succeeded in reorganizing the Downtown core around the massive Pacific Centre project; however, the conservationists defeated the freeway that would cut through the historic heart of the city.

In the 1970s, the pro-development promotion of skyscrapers and mega-projects that held sway during previous years was replaced by more community-based planning. Bank towers continued to multiply, but many projects, including Robson Square, Granville Island, False Creek, and Gastown, were built with a human scale. By the mid-eighties, the pendulum had swung back the other way. A new age of vigourous development was at hand, despite an economic recession that had landed more than 30,000 people out of work. The provincial government cut back on social programs and focused on the mega projects that would bring the world to Vancouver's doorstep for Expo 86. These included the multimillion dollar Canada Place Trade and Convention Centre, BC Place Stadium, and the SkyTrain light rapid transit system.

The 1980s were a defining decade for Vancouver. The age of the yuppie arrived with the proliferation of fitness gyms and condominiums.

But even after the hippies had been replaced by the yuppies, Vancouver preserved its activist roots. In the early 1980s, Vancouver declared itself a nuclear free zone, and established an annual Peace March that still attracts roughly 100,000 people every April.

Pacific Rim City

Beyond the consumer culture of the young professionals, more complex changes were transpiring. Vancouver was evolving into a more international, multiracial society than it ever had been. In the early eighties, Vancouver enjoyed the creation of some 200 new Chinese restaurants, and food critic Alex MacGillivray was quoted as saying: "If you

Opposite: In 1970, the founding members of Greenpeace met in an Oak Street church to plan their first protest against US nuclear tests in Amchitka. Since then, Vancouver has grown into a globally conscious centre. The annual Peace March began in 1981 and, today, draws over 100,000 participants each April. In 1982, Vancouver was declared a nuclear weapon free zone. These 1984 peace marchers are taking their message across the Burrard Street Bridge.

Top: This view illustrates the marriage of old and new. On the left is the old courthouse, built in 1910, and now home to the Vancouver Art Gallery. Behind it stands the third Hotel Vancouver, which was opened in 1939. The new Robson Square complex, designed by local architect Arthur Erickson in 1973, fills the centre. To the right are the many office buildings that sprang up downtown in the 1970s.

Middle: This statue lionizes Gastown's founding member, saloon-keeper "Gassy Jack" Deighton. When the commercial centre of the city moved west, Gastown sank into disrepair. The seventies introduced a revitalization program which saw Gastown's face brightened. Today, its cobblestone streets, old world atmosphere, and refubished warehouses make it a popular tourist attraction.

Bottom: When the first city council petitioned the government for Stanley Park in 1886, they predicted Vancouver's future as a great recreational centre. Every summer the city bursts with celebrations. The first Sea Festival, held in 1978, featured a bathtub race from Nanaimo to Vancouver.

Top: More remarkable than its natural beauty and the determination of its pioneers is the fact that Vancouver, Canada's third largest city, was built in the relatively short course of a hundred years.

Middle: When the distinctive, white dome of BC Place was inflated in 1983, it was the biggest self-supporting roof in the world. Home to the CFL's BC Lions, it seats 60,000. The new stadium heralded renewed interest in this portion of False Creek's shores. Industries like this sawmill were pushed out of False Creek in the early 1980s, when developers swooped down on the area.

Bottom: Vancouver celebrated its first centennial by hosting Expo 86, the World's Fair. Celebrated ocean-ographer Jacques Cousteau is here seen greeting fellow explorer Expo Ernie, the computerized mascot of the 1986 exhibition.

Opposite: The Canada Place complex was built in 1985 on the historical CPR Pier B-C, where many CPR cruiseship passengers were first introduced to Vancouver. In 1986, a new generation of visitors stopped here, when Pier B-C became the site of the Canada Pavilion for Expo 86. Today, this complex remains a dynamic focal point for the city. The five-sailed structure is the home of the Vancouver Trade and Convention Centre. The majestic Pan Pacific Hotel rises behind it.

want someone to credit for the fact that this has become a great restaurant town, you can thank the federal government's immigration policy." In 1960, 60 percent of Vancouverites were British in origin; but by 1989, 75 percent of Vancouver's foreign immigrants were arriving from Asia, and city schools counted some 60 languages being spoken by their students. By the end of the decade, Asian investment was contributing about $6 billion to BC's economy, with Japan becoming the Port of Vancouver's leading partner in trade.

1986 was the centennial of Vancouver, and a landmark year. The city reflected on the 100 years of work that had produced one of the country's most prosperous and diverse cities. In 1986, the shores of False Creek – an industrial wasteland just years earlier – were chosen as the site of the World's Fair. Expo 86 showcased the communication and transportation expertise of 100 different countries, and put Vancouver on the map for millions of foreign visitors. With the exposition, Vancouver revealed its aspirations to forge into the future as a world-class centre.

The years that followed brought a continuing stream of international visitors and investment. By 1989, readers of *Conde Nast Traveller Magazine* ranked Vancouver among their top 20 favourite cities in the world. The city's port became the leading foreign-tonnage handler in North America. The shores of False Creek were sold to Hong Kong developers and became the site of the largest real estate development on the continent. From its birth as a peaceful timber town in 1886, it was clear one century later that Vancouver had become a global city.

Photo Credits

Vancouver Public Library: 2, 5, 6, 8, 13, 14 top, 16, 17 bottom, 18 top, 20, 21, 22, 23, 24, 26, 27, 28, 29 top, 30, 33 bottom, 34, 35, 36, 37, 38 bottom, 39, 41, 42 bottom, 43, 44, 45 top and middle, 47, 49, 51, 52 bottom, 53, 54, 56, 58, 60 bottom, 62, 63, 65, 67 top, 68, 70, 71, 72, 73, 74, 75, 76, 77 bottom, 78, 80, 81, 82, 83, 84, 85, 86, 87, 88, 89, 90, 91 top, 93, 94, 95 top, 98, 99, 100, 101, 102, 104, 105 top and bottom, 106, 109, 110 top

City of Vancouver Archives: 10, 12, 17 top, 18 bottom, 25, 29 bottom, 32, 33 top, 38 top, 40, 42 top, 45 bottom, 46, 48, 50, 52 top, 55, 57, 59, 60 top, 61 bottom, 64, 66, 67 bottom, 77 top, 91 bottom, 92, 95 bottom, 105 middle, 108, 110 middle

Robert Keziere/Greenpeace: 107

Fred Herzog: 103

Jack Lindsay: 96

McCord Museum Archives: 14 bottom

Expo Corporation: 110 bottom, 111

Outside of four chilly years spent studying philosophy and literature at the University of Toronto, Aynsley Vogel has lived in Vancouver for twenty years. Her roots in the city stretch back four generations to the turn of the century when her great grandfather H.B.A. Vogel arrived in port from Denmark via Hawaii and San Francisco. Aynsley is a graduate of the Banff Publishing Workshop, and has worked as the volunteer coordinator at the Vancouver International Writers Festival.

Vancouver-born Dana Wyse is a freelance artist and writer. She was a contributing writer for *Vancouver SuperGuide*, and is currently working on her first novel.